SNOWY OWLS

by Melissa Hill

Consulting Editor:
Gail Saunders-Smith, PhD

Content Consultant:
Jessica Ehrgott,
Bird and Mammal Trainer,
Downtown Aquarium, Denver

CAPSTONE PRESS
a capstone imprint

Pebble Plus is published by Capstone Press,
1710 Roe Crest Drive, North Mankato, Minnesota 56003
www.capstonepub.com

Library of Congress Cataloging-in-Publication Data
Hill, Melissa, 1975– author.
Snowy Owls / by Melissa Hill.
pages cm.—(Pebble Plus. Owls)
Summary: "Simple text and full-color photographs describe
snowy owls"—Provided by publisher.
Audience: Ages 5–8.
Audience: K to grade 3.
Includes bibliographical references and index.
ISBN 978-1-4914-6048-1 (library binding)
ISBN 978-1-4914-6054-2 (paperback)
ISBN 978-1-4914-6068-9 (eBook pdf)
1. Snowy owl—Juvenile literature. I. Title.
QL696.S83H55 2015
598.9'7—dc23   2015005327

Editorial Credits

Jeni Wittrock, editor; Juliette Peters, designer; Morgan Walters, media researcher;
Katy LaVigne, production specialist

Photo Credits

Corbis: Kennan Ward, 17; Dreamstime: Brian Kushner, 9; Getty Images: mlorenzphotography,
22, Thomas Kokta, 15; Glow Images: ARCO /Wiede, U. & M., 19, Glenn Bartley, 5; iStockphoto:
bikec, 1; Science Source: Annie Haycock, 21; Shutterstock: Artography, Cover and throughout,
Artography, 3, 7, Dmitri Gomon, 3, LesPalenik, Cover, Maxim Petrichuk, 1, 2, 23, 24, MyImages-
Micha, 7, Paul Tessier, 11, J. Helgason, 2, 24; SuperStock: Bruce J Lichtenberge /Alaska Stock-
Design Pics, 13

Note to Parents and Teachers

The Owls set supports national curriculum standards for science related to life
science. This book describes and illustrates snowy owls. The images support
early readers in understanding the text. The repetition of words and phrases
helps early readers learn new words. This book also introduces early readers
to subject-specific vocabulary words, which are defined in the Glossary section.
Early readers may need assistance to read some words and to use the Table of
Contents, Glossary, Read More, Internet Sites, Critical Thinking Using the
Common Core, and Index sections of the book.

Printed in China by Nordica
0415/CA21500542
042015   008837NORDF15

Table of Contents

Great White Owls

A white owl with big, yellow eyes lands in the snow. Thick feathers keep her feet and body warm. She's a snowy owl.

Snowy owls are the largest owls in North America. Females can weigh more than 6 pounds (2.7 kilograms). Males are smaller.

Size Comparison

snowy owl	parakeet
length:	length:
20–28 inches	6–8 inches
(51–71 centimeters)	(15–20 centimeters)

Snowy Homes

Snowy owls begin their lives in the Arctic Circle. They are also found in North America, Europe, and Asia.

Snowy Owl Range Map

North America

South America

Europe

Asia

Africa

Australia

▨ where snowy owls live

Hidden Hunters

In snowy places, white feathers help snowy owls hide. They don't want their prey to see them. The owls' camouflage works well.

A hungry snowy owl listens for prey. Swoop! The owl's strong feet and sharp talons grab its prey. Snowy owls eat lemmings, voles, and other rodents.

If food is hard to find, snowy owls fly south. They may fly 2,000 miles (3,219 kilometers) or more. In spring they return to the Arctic Circle.

Arctic Families

In the Arctic, females scratch
a nest into the land. They lay
up to nine white eggs. A month
later, snowy owl chicks hatch.

Young snowy owls have fluffy white and gray feathers. Snowy owls take good care of their growing chicks.

In four months, the chicks can fly and hunt. As adults they will start families of their own. In the wild, snowy owls live about 10 years.

GLOSSARY

Arctic Circle—the area around the North Pole

camouflage—a color or pattern that helps an animal blend in with the things around it

chick—a young owl

hatch—to break out of an egg

prey—an animal that is hunted by other animals

predator—an animal that hunts other animals

rodent—one of a group of small mammals with large front teeth for chewing

talon—a long, sharp claw

READ MORE

Kim, Melissa & Jada Fitch. *A Snowy Owl Story.* Wildlife on the Move. Yarmouth, Maine: Islandport Press, 2015.

Murray, Julie. *Snowy Owls.* Arctic Animals. Minneapolis: ABDO Publishing Company, 2014.

Owen, Ruth. *Snowy Owls.* Polar Animals—Life in the Freezer. New York: Windmill Books, 2013.

INTERNET SITES

FactHound offers a safe, fun way to find Internet sites related to this book. All of the sites on FactHound have been researched by our staff.

Here's all you do:

Visit *www.facthound.com*

Type in this code: 9781491460481

Check out projects, games and lots more at
www.capstonekids.com

CRITICAL THINKING USING THE COMMON CORE

1. Why are snowy owls' feathers important?
(Key Ideas and Details)

2. Why do you think female snowy owls are larger than males?
(Integration of Knowledge and Ideas)

INDEX

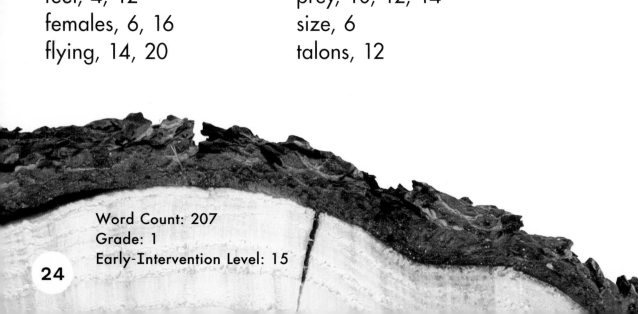

Word Count: 207
Grade: 1
Early-Intervention Level: 15